Native Americans

Great Basin Indians

Mir Tamim Ansary

Heinemann Library
Des Plaines, Illinois

© 2000 Reed Educational & Professional Publishing
Published by Heinemann Library,
an imprint of Reed Educational & Professional Publishing,
Chicago, IL

Customer Service: 888-454-2279

Visit our website at www.heinemannlibrary.com

Printed in Hong Kong
Designed by Depke Design

05 04 03 02 01
10 9 8 7 6 5 4 3 2

Library of Congress Cataloging-in-Publication Data
Ansary, Mir Tamim.
　　Great Basin Indians / Mir Tamim Ansary.
　　　　p. cm. – (Native Americans)
　　Includes bibliographical references.
　　Summary: Introduces the various Native American tribes of the
Great Basin region, discussing their history, dwellings, artwork,
religious beliefs, clothing, food, and other aspects of their way of
life.
　　ISBN 1-57572-922-9 (lib. bdg.)　　　　　　ISBN 1-58810-452-4 (pbk. bdg.)
　　1. Indians of North America—Great Basin—History Juvenile
literature. 2. Indians of North America—Great Basin—Social life
and customs Juvenile literature. [1. Indians of North America—
Great Basin.] I. Title. II. Series: Ansary, Mir Tamim. Native
Americans.
E78.G67A67   1999
979.004'97—dc21　　　　　　　　　　99-21261
　　　　　　　　　　　　　　　　　　　　　　CIP

Acknowledgments
The publisher would like to thank the following for permission to reproduce photographs:
Cover: Photo Researchers, Inc./John Eastcott/Yva Momatiuk
Photo Researchers, Inc./Robert Bornemann, pp. 4, 5; Edward S. Curtis/National Geographic, pp. 6, 12; Photo Researchers,
Inc./Gilbert S. Grant, p. 8; Dr. E.R. Degginger, pp. 9, 10, 11; North Wind Pictures, pp. 13, 15, 17, 21; James L. Amos/National
Geographic, p. 14; Bridgeman Art Library International Ltd., pp. 16, 18, 24; Lawrence Migdale, pp. 19, 20, 23; Bruce
Dale/National Geographic, p. 22; Bridgeman Art Library International Ltd./Oscar Beringhaus, p. 25; The Granger Collection,
pp. 26, 30; The Granger Collection/Frederic Remington, p. 27; Photo Researchers, Inc./U.S. Department of Energy, p. 28; Photo
Researchers, Inc./John Eastcott/Yva Momatiuk, p. 29.

Every effort has been made to contact copyright holders of any material reproduced in this book.
Any omissions will be rectified in subsequent printings if notice is given to the publisher.

Our special thanks to Lola Grant, Native American MLS, for
her expertise in the preparation of this book.

Note to the Reader Some words are shown in bold, **like this.** You can find
out what they mean by looking in the glossary.

Contents

The Great Basin

Much of Utah and Nevada is shaped like a big washtub or basin. It is low, flat land surrounded by mountains. Rivers that flow into this "Great Basin" never reach the ocean. They dry up or trickle into salty lakes and big **marshes.**

The Great Basin is very hot in the summer and freezing cold in winter. It doesn't rain much here. The soil is salty, which makes farming almost impossible. This is a hard place for people to live. Yet people have lived in this desert for a long time.

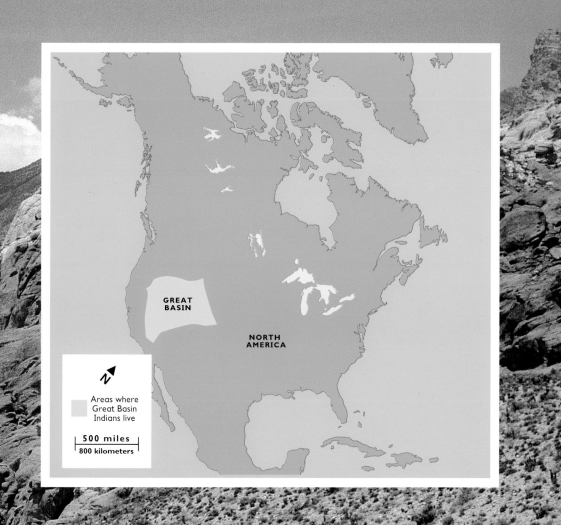

GREAT BASIN

NORTH AMERICA

Areas where Great Basin Indians live

500 miles
800 kilometers

The First People

People have lived in the Great Basin for at least ten thousand years. No one knows where they came from. Perhaps they were crowded out of the Great Plains. They spread across the Great Basin in tiny groups, hunting and gathering. Their way of life changed very little until Europeans came to America in the 1500s.

This man belonged to the Paviotso tribe. His band was called the "black-sucker eaters."

By then, five main tribes were sharing this region. They were the Shoshone, the Utes, the Paiutes, the Bannock, and the Washo. The Washo spoke a language called Hokan. All the others spoke Shoshone or a language that came from Shoshone. They all followed a very similar way of life.

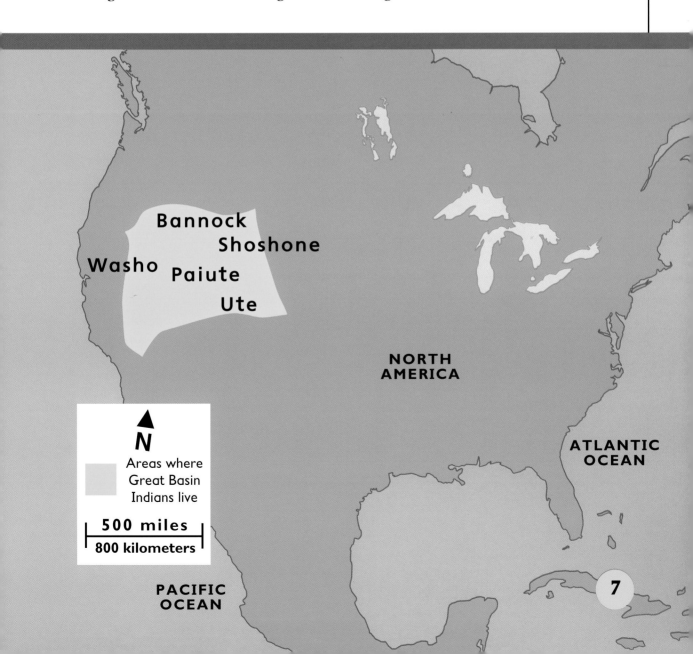

Bannock

Shoshone

Washo Paiute

Ute

NORTH AMERICA

ATLANTIC OCEAN

N

Areas where Great Basin Indians live

500 miles

800 kilometers

PACIFIC OCEAN

Gathering and Hunting

Native Americans of the Great Basin mostly ate wild plants. No one kind of plant was plentiful. So people gathered about 75 different kinds of plants. They ate nuts and roots and berries. They ate seeds and **shoots** and **bulbs.** Pine nuts were among their favorite foods.

These pine nuts come from the piñon pine, a bushlike tree.

Jackrabbits live in great numbers in the Great Basin.

The people of the Great Basin were hunters, too. They hunted everything from insects to prairie dogs. They used fire to bring down grasshoppers, which they toasted and ate. They herded antelopes into **corrals** of **brush.** The animal they hunted most, however, was the jackrabbit.

Living on the Move

Since food was **scarce,** people could not live in one place. They traveled in family groups of two to twenty people. Each family followed a pattern throughout the year. In the spring, the family gathered **bulbs** along valley streams. Then the group moved across the meadows, gathering grass seeds and hunting rabbits.

When streams like this one in Utah dried up in late summer, family groups living nearby were forced to move.

*This **juniper** tree has berries that ripen in late summer.*

In the fall, the family started moving up the mountains. Nuts and berries ripen later as one goes higher. So people kept coming to newly ripe food as they climbed. They ate some of this food. They dried some for the winter. When the weather cooled, they moved down to a **sheltered** place.

Group Hunts and Gatherings

Usually, each family group traveled alone. Once or twice a year, many families gathered in one place. The Washo met at Lake Tahoe each spring to catch fish. The Paiutes held a rabbit drive each fall. Hundreds of people worked together to herd rabbits into a net. The Utes had antelope drives.

Fish were caught with hooks made from bone, nets, and double-pointed spears, like this one.

Paiute stories say that Coyote, pictured here, created the world.

These gatherings were times of fun. People sang
and danced. Marriages were set up. The elders told
stories about characters such as Coyote. Coyote
was a naughty trickster. He was clever, magical, sly,
and well-loved. Coyotes were among the few
animals no one in the Great Basin ate.

Shelter in the Great Basin

Like most **nomads,** the people of the Great Basin built no lasting houses. In the summer, they often slept in the open. Sometimes they built a lean-to as a wind shelter. A lean-to is like one leaning wall. The frame is made of branches. **Brush** is piled over this frame.

This Shoshone family was photographed in their lean-to in 1871, somewhere in Idaho.

Wikiups were made throughout the deserts of the Great Basin and the Southwest.

In winter, up to fifteen families lived together in a village of wikiups. A wikiup is a cone-shaped hut. **Juniper** tree branches make up the frame. Brush, bark, or woven grass is laid over the frame. A firepit in the middle provides heat. A hole above the pit lets out smoke.

Clothing in the Great Basin

Long ago, people of the Great Basin made their clothing from wild plants. Women wore aprons made from milkweed plants. Men wore **breechcloths** made from this plant. The Paiutes and Washo used willow tree bark to weave hats that looked like baskets. These hats protected them from strong sunlight.

This medicine man is wearing a type of short skirt called a kilt.

These Utes lived in southern Colorado around 1800.

In the winter, people wore rabbit skin robes. They stitched many skins together to make these robes. But in the 1800s, after white settlers came to this area, clothing styles changed. The Native Americans traded for items such as pants, dresses, and boots. They started dressing like Europeans.

Baskets for Many Purposes

Some of the world's first baskets were made in the Great Basin. Baskets were perfect containers for **nomads** because they were light and strong. People used baskets to gather foods and sift seeds. The baskets were so tightly woven, they were like jars—they could hold water.

The people of the Great Basin wove fine baskets out of reeds and grasses.

Thanks to the leather straps, this basket could be worn like a backpack.

Baskets were even used for cooking in the Great Basin. A basket was filled with water. Then red-hot stones were dropped into it. Each stone made the water hotter. At last the water in the basket started boiling. Then soup and other food could be cooked in it.

People Without Rulers

The Great Basin tribes had no real **governments.** They didn't need any because people lived so far apart. But families met and mingled as they wandered. Stories, news, and customs spread through a tribe. The people in each family felt like they belonged to a larger group.

Indian elders still pass stories and wisdom down to children by word of mouth.

The rabbit boss helped keep a big rabbit hunt organized.

The wisest people were called "talkers." Talkers called families together for group hunts. During the hunt, the talker acted as a chief. The leader of a Paiute rabbit drive, for example, was called the rabbit boss. But after the drive, each family went its own way.

Shamans and Sweat Lodges

The people of the Great Basin thought dreams were important. Men and women who had powerful dreams became shamans. The shaman is still a respected person in many Indian communities. Shamans are supposed to be able to heal people who are ill. The Utes believed their shamans could also dream where to hunt for antelopes.

A shaman's ceremonies are meant to drive away spirits that cause illness.

Another way to keep away illness was the sweat bath. Men still gather in sweat lodges for this religious ceremony. The sweat lodge is a hut without windows. Hot stones are passed into the hut until the men are sweating freely. The sweat bath is thought to make a person pure inside.

These modern-day Indians are about to use a sweat lodge they have built.

A Way of Life Ends

The Spanish brought horses to America in the 1500s. Some horses got away. Over time, wild horses spread across America. By the 1600s, many Utes and Shoshones had horses, which changed their way of life. They began roaming onto the plains to hunt buffalo. They began to **raid** other tribes, too.

The horse changed Native American life throughout the West.

The Gold Rush brought thousands of covered wagons through the Great Basin.

In 1848, gold was found in California. Settlers and miners streamed across the Great Basin. They trampled plants the Native Americans needed to survive. The settlers killed **scarce** game and attacked peaceful people such as the Paiutes. The Native Americans of this region began to suffer.

Whites Take Over

The Utes and Bannock tried to fight back. But they could not stand up to the guns of the U.S. Army. They were forced onto **reservations.** So were tribes that tried to keep the peace. Some were sent far from their homes in Utah and Nevada to reservations in Idaho and Wyoming.

Shoshone leader Washakie kept the peace but fought for his people's rights.

The Ghost Dance spread all the way to South Dakota, where these Sioux Indians lived.

In 1888, a Paiute named Wovoka brought back a religion that had died out in the 1860s. He preached that whites would disappear and dead Indians would rise again. Indians could help by dancing a special "ghost dance." This message spread to the plains. It started one last wave of Indian wars. But in 1890, the U.S. Army crushed these warriors at Wounded Knee Creek in South Dakota.

The Great Basin Tribes Today

Today, Native Americans of the Great Basin have **reservations** from Nevada to Wyoming. They make money from ranching, farming, or tourism. But the reservations have problems. For example, **nuclear bombs** have been tested near these lands. The Shoshone have gone to **court** to stop these tests.

Some nuclear bombs are exploded underground. This is a test site in Nevada. The cables here are connected to underground equipment.

A young Shoshone does a "fancy dance" for visitors at South Pass City, Wyoming.

Two or more tribes share some reservations. For example, the Shoshone and Bannock share the Fort Hall Reservation in Idaho. They now call themselves the Sho-Bans. Once a year, they host a huge "Indian **Festival**." Both Indian and non-Indian visitors come to this festival to relive memories of times past.

Famous Great Basin Indians

Wovoka (Paiute: 1856–1932) Wovoka was the shaman who brought back the Ghost Dance religion. His teachings came to him in a dream around 1888. His message was one of peace, love, and sharing. But Wovoka's message changed as it spread. It became a call to war.

Sarah Winnemucca (Paiute: 1844–1891) Winnemucca served as a scout for the U.S. Army. Later, she went to Washington, D.C., to speak for her people. She protested how the U.S. **government** was mistreating them. Her book *Life Among the Paiutes* described how the Paiutes were suffering.

Washakie (Shoshone: 1804–1900) Washakie became famous as a warrior. Yet he worked hard for peace with the white settlers. He helped get a large **reservation** for his people at Wind River, Wyoming. He also got the U.S. government to pay the Shoshone for the lands they had lost.

Glossary

breechcloth cloth that is passed between the legs and over a belt hanging down like an apron in back and front

brush thick growth of weeds and shrubs mixed with broken branches

bulb round, hard underground part of a plant; for example, an onion

corral fenced-in place into which animals can be herded

court place where crimes and quarrels are judged according to the law

festival big public party celebrating something

government organized group that makes laws and keeps order

juniper type of evergreen tree with prickly branches

marsh low land that is wet and soft, often with plants growing in it

nomad person who travels from place to place and has no permanent home

nuclear bomb very powerful bomb that causes much damage and can make people sick long after it's exploded

preached spoke out to give a religious message

raid to attack quickly and suddenly, often to steal goods from people

reservation land set aside for Native Americans.

scarce hard to find; not plentiful

sheltered protected from wind, rain, and other bad weather

shoot young leaf, bud, or branch of a plant

More Books to Read

Carter, Alden R. *The Shoshoni.* Danbury, Conn.: Franklin Watts Incorporated, 1989.

McLerran, Alice. *The Ghost Dance.* New York: Houghton Mifflin Company, 1995.

Index